W9-BPD-131

GOD
made easy

PATRICE KARST

CEDAR MILL PRESS
BOOK PUBLISHERS

KENNEBUNKPORT, MAINE

13-Digit ISBN: 978-1-933662-87-9
10-Digit ISBN: 1-933662-87-5

This book may be ordered by mail from the publisher. Please include $2.00 for postage and handling. Please support your local bookseller first!

Books published by Cider Mill Press Book Publishers are available at special discounts for bulk purchases in the United States by corporations, institutions, and other organizations. For more information, please contact the publisher.

Cider Mill Press Book Publishers   "Where good books are ready for press"
12 Port Farm Road, Kennebunkport, Maine 04046

Visit us on the web at www.cidermillpress.com

Design by Jessica Disbrow
Printed in Thailand

1 2 3 4 5 6 7 8 9 0
First Edition

Dedicated to the
hope and vision that
all beings, in all worlds,
will one day be happy.

Foreword

REINCARNATION, when it comes to humans, is a matter of debate. In the case of books, we know it sometimes takes place. It's happened for *God Made Easy*, and that is something to celebrate.

I discovered the earlier edition of this book in the late 1990s. It was breathtaking at the time to read such a tiny, elegant encapsulation of what Aldous Huxley called the "perennial philosophy." Here was an explanation of God that bypassed dogma and doctrine, and went straight to the Source ---literally. Like the mystics of all times and cultures, Patrice Karst got it ---and she was generous enough to share her enlightenment with the rest of us in a way that left no one out. My husband, a self-professed agnostic, appreciated this book. So did the friends---including a Catholic priest, a Baptist minister, and a Conservative rabbi---to whom I gave copies as gifts.

In rereading this little gem a decade later, *God Made Easy* is just as meaningful and even more relevant. Religious turmoil---basically a misunderstanding of the nature of God---is at the root of most of the wars and terrorist acts wreaking havoc across the globe. It also contributes substantially to the unpleasantness that occurs all around us every day: red states versus blue states; mainstream Christians versus the ones with all the TV programs; the people who were born here versus those who came from somewhere else, bringing with them their "odd" beliefs and their "strange" God.

In her beautiful description of the Divine, by whatever name you wish to call Him, Her, or It, Patrice Karst implants in the soul of her readers ideas that could alter the fate of this planet. Among them: God is bigger than your differences. God loves all of you. And He'd like it if you'd look at His other children and see their resemblance to Him---even if they don't see yours. Yet.

Reading *God Made Easy* may well heal parts of yourself you'd thought would be ailing for the duration. And when it does, your light will shine brightly enough to change your life---and maybe the world while you're at it.

--Victoria Moran, author of *Fat, Broke & Lonely No More,* and *Creating a Charmed Life*. You can visit her at www.victoriamoran.com.

Introduction

IN THIS OH-SO-BAFFLING AND CONFUSING WORLD in which we live, I have spent my life in search of the answers to the mysteries of the universe, some sense of understanding. This deep need to explore the spiritual realms, along with a love of writing and speaking, led me on a quest that has been an incredible journey - not always easy, but fascinating, to say the least. From ashrams in India to workshops in California, I continued praying and meditating that God would reveal to me the true nature of the spiritual worlds, and what it all meant. Along the way, I indeed was fortunate to experience and see things that absolutely blew my western rational mind. Miracles that challenged all of my belief systems; beings and visions that would appear and instruct me in my dreams and half-awake states; holy ones who knew things about me that were "impossible" for them to know. After a while I knew beyond any shadow of a doubt that the world as I knew it was but a tiny glimmer of what was really out there.

Along the journey, so very many amazing things occurred. I was now the single mother of a wonderful child named Elijah. Working a full-time job and living by the ocean in Los Angeles, I continued to study all of the esoteric, spiritual, metaphysical and new-age teachings I could get my hands on, and wrote about my hopes, fears, dreams and gripes - the struggles of being a seeker living in crazy times on our planet Earth - always wishing I could figure out what was my true life's work. Then, the miracle.........

On the morning of November 11, 1995, at six a.m., I was awoken from a dream. Elijah was still sound asleep and I was quite groggy, yet there - plain as day in giant, bold letters right in front of my eyes - were the words, *God Made Easy*. I had absolutely no idea why I was seeing this, but I remember thinking, "What a great book title!" And trying to go back to sleep. The only way I can describe what happened next was that I was absolutely not allowed to drift off again. From deep within me came a command, "Get up and write it now!!" Let me add here that this did not thrill me; as a sleep-deprived single mom, I cherished my rest. Still, thank God, I reluctantly did as told, grabbed a spiral notebook and started to write. What occurred next was a most extraordinary experience. The words began to pour out of me. There was no pausing, thinking, or rewriting - just a stream of consciousness that spilled out faster than I could get it down. At exactly seven a.m., it was done. In just one hour I was holding in my hands a piece of writing that, upon reading, gave me goose bumps [God bumps]. The voice spoke again: "This is to be a book. It will go all over the world reaching and reintroducing all the people of this planet to the great magnificence that is God. Whether they are 10 or 110 years old, Buddhist, Jew, Christian, or no particular belief at all, this tiny book will simplify once and for all everything that we need to know about life here on Earth, Heaven, God and how to be happy. And now Patrice, your job is to get it published."

At this point I couldn't tell if I was completely deluding myself or if indeed Spirit had finally revealed to me what my mission in life really was. If I had known then what I now know about the correct protocol of trying to get a book published, I might have given up. Luckily for me, however, my ignorance was bliss as I simply, naively went into a bookstore, wrote down the names of three publishers that had spiritual books, and proceeded to call them on the telephone. Introducing myself, I informed them that I had written a mass market book about God, and that I had been told to get it published. [I at least had the savvy not to tell them Who told me to get it published!]

Less than a month later I was sitting at a restaurant in Marina Del Rey, California, signing my first publishing deal with De Vorss, a metaphysical publisher in Los Angeles. I was elated. I had done what I was told, and my book was on its way to bookstore heaven. The rest has been an unfolding miracle beyond my grandest dreams. A few weeks later, *God Made Easy* was sold to TimeWarner Books, one of the biggest publishing houses in the world. Ellen Burstyn [one of my favorite actresses] did the reading for the audio version, which has been translated into French, Dutch and Spanish, and has sold over 50,000 copies - making its way, one person at a time, around the world. Showers of grace, one after the other have opened the doors that this little tiny book with the BIG message can soar and, ultimately perhaps, even fly to you.

By far the best part of this whole adventure has been the chance to talk to so many people everywhere about my favorite topic of conversation, God. The letters I have received from people around the country that have been touched by this book have brought tears to my eyes and joy to my heart. From convicts, drug addicts and suicidal teenagers, to CEO's, rabies and housewives, ages 6 to 96.

Now, so many years later, I am thrilled to have the opportunity to republish this book that it can reach a world that needs its message now more than ever. I have been given the great honor and privilege to bring forth and share this message: That God is here for us all, no matter what name we choose to call Him, Her, It, and that we are Loved! The search continues still, from joyful moments of seeming enlightenment to dark despair and feelings of hopelessness. Certain universal truths have made themselves clear to me, and from them comes a wonderful sense of comfort and a knowing of their ultimate validity.

May we together embrace both our individual searches for God and respect the different roads we all take to reach the peak called Home. May we laugh together often, cry less, and, as brothers and sisters in this glorious global family, celebrate the search together.

God bless us all,
Patrice Karst

GOD
made easy

PATRICE KARST

IN CASE YOU HAVEN'T NOTICED

The world is feeling pretty crazy lately on every level...

Environmental nightmares
and natural disasters

Crime, crime, crime

Hate, hate, hate

Economic strife

Drug addictions, alcoholism

Technology advancing so
fast you can't keep up

Wars, starvation, AIDS,
vanishing bees

We're running on a treadmill that's going faster and faster.

CHANGES ARE HAPPENING

....

Has all of this gotten
your attention yet?

It's time to remember
who you really are
once again...

HEY, WHOA, STOP!

There's good stuff, too!

Yep, you're right, it's all here on planet Earth.

Just to name a few:

RAINBOWS

SHOOTING STARS

BABIES

SEX

HOT FUDGE

THE GRAND CANYON

GOOD COMEDY

You get the idea...

BUT GUESS WHAT?

....

There's SOMEONE who's
gotten really bad press
all these years - in fact,
a lot of us can't even
say the name without a
bunch of religious dogma
pouring through us.

(None of which has anything to do
with Him, Her, It - whatever name you
choose, by the way.)

And maybe during
all this insanity
it's time we all got
reacquainted; in fact,
maybe that's been
part of the problem...

...Forgetting...

INTRODUCING

....

once again,
back by popular
demand -

and need...

GOD

Wait! Before you get all charged up and your buttons pushed out of shape, the great news about God is that He* has absolutely no ego and will be perfectly content if you wish to call Him instead...

(*He, She, it whatever you're comfortable with...read on.)

GODDESS

SUPREME BEING

HEAVENLY FATHER
(or even Big Dad)

DIVINE MOTHER

THE CREATOR

LORD

HOLY SPIRIT

HIGHER POWER

THE MAN UPSTAIRS

A LOVING PRESENCE

(there's more)

ALMIGHTY

INFINITE INTELLIGENCE

UNIVERSAL ENERGY

COSMIC CONSCIOUSNESS

THE LIGHT WITHIN

THE SOURCE

THE FORCE

SOMETHING BIGGER THAN ME

YOU GET THE IDEA

Just fill in the blank with any name you want.

_____

(Just fill in the blank!)

TRUST ME.
You'll have a better life.

AND HERE'S SOME MORE GOOD NEWS

No religion or spiritual path has an exclusive with God; He is the ultimate independent contractor.

Therefore, even if
you hear Him called...

GAIA (Mother Earth)

ALLAH

KRISHNA

BUDDHA

LAKSHMI

CHRIST

GREAT SPIRIT

SHIVA

KUAN-YIN

RAMA

JEHOVAH

KALI

ADONAI

and the many others...

THEY'RE ALL TRUE, AND IT'S ALL OK

....

One God -
many different names.

Don't worry, He has
absolutely no problem
with this, just some
fearful, bossy people who
feel it's their job to tell you
who God is - or isn't.

SO HOW DO YOU GET TO KNOW THIS GOD ANYWAY?

....

Now the fun begins...

Oh, and by the way: the less intellect here, the better. To find God, you've got to get real simple.

What's really
great is
that God is
everywhere...

...and there's
nowhere that
He isn't...

One place you can start if you're into reading is "The books."

Once again, folks, no one book has the only true story, the only right truth.

Some possibilities...

THE BIBLE

THE KORAN

THE TORAH

THE BAGAVAD GITA

THE UPANISHADS

And various spiritual,
metaphysical, or mystical/
esoteric titles

THOUGH:

Books can give you an idea, but to really get up close and personal, you've gotta get your head outta the books and into...

....

You'll see God and His
handiwork all over. Every
bird, rock, tree, stream.
Hey, have you ever really
looked at a flower? Get
quiet; you'll here Him in
the silence.

BABIES

Just hang out with babies or small children, get real goofy with them and let go. Voila! God.

GOING INSIDE

Start a running dialog with Him. He is, after all, the nearest and dearest. Just start talking to, crying to, singing to, laughing with, asking why, praying to Him (no formality needed); just take the plunge next time you're feeling sad or scared or lonely. Trust He is listening and tell Him what's up...

Then, and this is real important: Shut up and

LISTEN!

It doesn't matter where you are - in bed, at the bus stop, making up your kid's lunchbox - anywhere. Or if you want to get real fancy, make an altar, light a candle, burn incense, put groovy holy pictures up and meditate. The point is, expect to hear Him; then get quiet and give him a chance to respond.

CHURCHES, TEMPLES, SHRINES, SACRED SPOTS

....

Lots of good God energy going on here.

GREAT MUSIC, ART, WRITINGS

....

Ain't no way, nohow, a human can create that without some kind of help from above.

CASE CLOSED.

ACTS of KINDNESS, LOVE, and SUPPORT

When we humans are at our best and our hearts are all warm and fuzzy inside... that's when you know Who is at work again!

YOUR OWN CONSCIENCE

You know that inner stuff that says Uh-oh! Don't do that! Or Stay away from him or Gosh! She looks like she could use a hug!

Well, guess Who's prompting you?

THE BREATH

....

No science allowed, please
(it has its place, but in the
grand scheme of things,
unbelievably limited). Guess
what? Twenty-four hours a
day SOMETHING is making
that heart of yours pump in
and is breathing your lungs in
and out, in and out... Follow
it back inside.

MIRACLES

The phone call that comes at the perfect second. Being rescued at the last moment. Those "impossible" coincidences that give you goosebumps (God bumps).

Start watching for them: you'll see even more.

FOOD

There has got to be something pretty wonderful in charge of things that grow out of dirt that taste that good.

Period!

ANIMALS

The colors, varieties,
sounds, shapes - all living,
breathing, sharing our world.

Who do you think
made 'em?

So why
all the
bad stuff?

I know, I know;
if there really
is a God,
why all the crap?
All the suffering?

Good
question...

Karma... Balance... Lessons to Learn

....

Somewhere, sometime,
somehow, for every action
there was and is a reaction.
Also known as "What you
sow, you shall reap," or cause
and effect. Not always fun,
sometimes downright painful,
excruciating, yucky...

...Doesn't mean you can't get mad, pissed off, at
God. He doesn't even mind if you scream at Him
(remember, no ego).

Perhaps a lot of it remains a mystery until the very end; perhaps we can't understand it all right now with our limited human minds... You just have to trust that there is order in the universe and that all will make sense eventually (what else are you going to do?).

Earth is a school, a place we come to learn what we need to so we finally get it right, graduate once and for all, and go somewhere else...

AND NOW THE BEST PART OF ALL

....

We're going home!!!!

This does not mean that you don't enjoy the ride down here on Earth to its fullest. It just means there's something really big to look forward to...

Call it what you want...

HEAVEN

NIRVANA

SHANGRI-LA

BLISS

ASTRAL PLANE

"OVER THERE"

SPIRIT WORLD

THE OTHER SIDE

THE GREAT BEYOND

FROM WHENCE I CAME

Oh, and by the way - the whole "hell" thing: Unless you've been the worst, most murderous, hideous, evil monster that ever lived, I really wouldn't worry about it...

And even if you were, everyone eventually is given a chance to rehabilitate...

WORST CASE:

If you weren't great in this life, you might have to come back and do it all over again...

...maybe.

SO, NOW,
imagine a place with...

No suffering - NONE!

No physical illness or injuries

No death

No questions unanswered

No longing not met

Color, smells, sights, and
sounds that are more
beautiful than your wildest
imaginings

Being able to go from here
to there anywhere in the
cosmos at will

Seeing and being with all
you've ever loved

Hanging out with GOD on a
daily basis... effortlessly

Being happy all the time

Doing and learning whatever
you want

No cold, no fears, no tears...

WAIT JUST A MINUTE!

....

"Sounds too good to be true; can't be," you say. "Who the heck is this girl and how can she make a promise like this?"

"Anyway, how dare she?"

Well, guess what: It's all true. Absolutely, every word. I can't prove it to you. This is where that concept of "faith" comes in. But quite simply, this has been the message since the beginning of time... We're only here on Earth for a short while and then we go home... and home is incredible...

So if I'm wrong... sue me!
(You won't need to.)

Okay, so what to do while we're still here?

Real simple. Read on...

Be kind to all...

especially to yourself. The Golden
Rule applies here (also known as
"Do unto others as you would have
them do unto you"). All religions
and languages have their version
of this rule, by the way. It's a
universal thing.

Find and get to know God...

Your own heart is the best place to
start.

Have fun...

There's a lot to do, be, and see here;
you might as well make the most
out of the visit. And as they say,
you only go around once (at least in
this body).

Care about what matters...

Hint: at the end you won't remember or care much about the money you made, but you will remember and care about who you loved and who loved you back. This will become obvious when you start tuning in...

Just remember, all you can take with you is who you became and what you learned on your journey. The rest is maya - illusion.

Be authentic - speak your truth...

God created you to be uniquely different from anyone else. He had reasons; don't mess with the program.

Try to develop a new "attitude of gratitude"...

When you start to see your life in this way, you'll be amazed at how different it can look.

Don't hold grudges...

Life really is too short; Forgiveness is a good thing (and anyway, it feels better!).

Hang out in the "present"...

not the future or the past. Each moment is His gift. (Why do you think it's called "the present"?)

Start to surrender...

You may know this as "Thy will be done" or "Let go and let God." The fact is that He who created butterfly wings and the Himalayan Mountains knows His stuff - you may want to let Him lead for a change.

Look for the lessons...

Learn all you can... get wise... Stay humble.

Lastly, look toward the journey home...

Your soul, your being, is here for all eternity...   ...So don't sweat the small stuff.

God bless

Peace be with you

Enjoy the ride

Shalom

Hallelujah

Namaste

Walk in grace and beauty

Om

Peace

Amen

...and maybe, just maybe, if we each do our part (and with a little help from Him), this wonderful spinning blue orb on which we all find ourselves can finally heal.

....

Remember...

We're all in
this together...

...more will
be revealed...

and never,
ever forget...

you are loved...

There is no end...

PATRICE KARST has quickly become one of the most well-loved and refreshing spiritual voices out there. Using her unique blend of humor, honesty, audience interaction, and profound wisdom, she shares her message of hope, inspiration, and comfort to appreciative audiences everywhere, and has been featured on television shows across the country, including *CSPAN*, *ABC* and *Fox News*, as well as on hundreds of radio shows, and in newspapers and magazines.

A spiritual seeker since childhood, her quest culminated in the writing of *God Made Easy*. The book has touched the hearts and souls of people from every age, religion, and walk of life worldwide. Hers is a miraculous story: On the morning of November 11, 1995, she was awoken from a dream and "told" to write her book. She did it in an hour and signed a deal to have it published three weeks later! Her book has been praised by John Grey *Men Are from Mars-Women Are from Venus*, Barbara De Angelis *Real Moments*, and Larry Dossey, M.D. *Prayer is Good Medicine*, among others. She has also written *The Single Mother's Survival Guide; The Invisible String*; and *The Smile That Went Around the World*.

Patrice lives in Los Angeles with her family, including, her "weiner dog," Coco. When not touring and writing, she works as a spirituality counselor at renowned drug and alcohol treatment centers in Malibu, and is producing her first feature film. You can write to her at PatriceKarst@aol.com or P.O. Box 2606, Malibu, CA 90265. She would love to hear from you.